Drift Migration

Dear Michaella,
So wonderful to meet with you
in Cedar City! Hope you find
Some images of landscape
that will resonent with a
sense of place!
Danielle

Drift Migration

poems

❧

Danielle Beazer Dubrasky

Danielle Beazer Dubrasky

THE ASHLAND POETRY PRESS

Printed in the United States of America
ISBN: 978-0-912592-95-4
Library of Congress Card Catalogue Number: 2021941587

Author Photo: Kurtis Leany
Cover art: Diane Walsh, *Nocturne*, Artisans Art Gallery
Cover design: Nicholas Fedorchak
Book layout: Mark E. Cull
Editing: Jennifer Rathbun and Deborah Fleming

Acknowledgments

Many thanks to the editors and presses below, wherein these poems first appeared, sometimes in slightly different form or with different titles:

15 Bytes: "The ceiling fan spins your childhood"
Blossom as the Cliffrose: "Evensong"
Cave Wall Press: "Heliography," "Palimpsest," "Snow in March"
Chiron Review: "One Shot"
Contrary Magazine: "Clouds turn from white to gray to black," "Deer tongue fallen apples," "She speaks on your last morning," "So many flowers," "What she has given you," "Your treasures are marbles"
Fire in the Pasture (anthology): "Great Basin"
Hoppermag.org/contest-winners: "Venus"
Invisible Shores (letterpress folio, Red Butte Press): "Great Basin" (re-print), "Metamorphic"
Irreantum: "Drift Migration," "Leaving Virginia"
Kolob Canyon Review: "Desert Insomnia"
Limberlost Review: "Shadow Prints"
Open: Journal of Arts & Letters: "Hollow Bones," "Kaleidoscope"
Petroglyph: "Night the trees trill at the edge of my ear"
Pilgrimage: "Memory at Taylor Creek"
Quill and Parchment: "She looks for the day," "When she first lay beside you"
saltfront: "Retrieval" (in print journal and as a broadside)
South Dakota Review: "Circadian," "Ghost Flower," "Lighting Out for the Invisible," "Vivarium"
Sugar House Review: "Petroglyphs at Parowan Gap," "The Sand Man," "Vespers in the Great Basin"
Terrain.org: "Sepulveda Basin Refuge," "Winter Solstice in the Gorge"
Torrey House Press Blog: "Flight Path"
Under a Warm Green Linden: "The Glass Blower"
Utah@125: "All Fever Gone"
Weber Studies: "Leda," "Quietus"

The following poems from "Eurydice's Mirror" were published in the chapbook *Ruin and Light*, winner of the Anabiosis Press 2014 Chapbook Competition: "The ceiling fan spins your childhood," "Your treasures are marbles," "The children who have never heard rain," "She once fell asleep to a river," "Deer tongue fallen apples," "She carries a sundial shell," "She sleeps in the folds of your shirt," "She uncovers antler bone," "She speaks on your last morning," "So many flowers," "When she first lay beside you," "What she has given you," "She looks for the day," "Clouds turn from white to gray to black."

"Circadian" won Second Place in the 2018 Utah Arts Council Original Writing Competition for Poetry, and "The Sand Man" won First Place in the 2011 Utah Arts Council Original Writing Competition for Poetry.

"Palimpsest" won Honorable Mention in the 2017 Cave Wall Press National Broadside Competition.

"Night the trees trill at the edge of my ear" won Second Place in the 2000 Original Writing Contest in *Petroglyph*, from Utah State University, published as "Grotto."

Poems from "Blood-Red Seeds" were first published in 2003 as a chapbook *Persephone Awakened* by Woodhenge Press.

Versions of this manuscript have been recognized as a finalist or semi-finalist at the following competitions: 42 Miles Press, Able-Muse Press, Ashland Poetry Press, Backwaters Press, Crab Orchard Review, Elixir Press, The Hopper Press, Howling Bird Press, and Galileo Press.

Many thanks to the readers and friends who reviewed early versions of these poems and offered so much insight and encouragement: Wyn Cooper, Nancy Takacs, Geraldine Connolly, Natasha Saje, Mark Irwin, Jennifer Tonge, Robin Calland, and Ruth Scoville.

I want to give a special thank you to my teachers and mentors: Simone Di Piero, Donald Revell, Jacqueline Osherow, Mark Doty, Ken Fields, and the late Leslie Norris.

I appreciate The Virginia Center for Creative Arts for providing a place of such beauty and inspiration that allowed me to complete "The Sand Man" and "Eurydice's Mirror."

I wish to express deep gratitude to Deborah Fleming and Ashland Poetry Press.

I have eternal gratitude to friends and astute readers Nano Taggart and Natalie Young, whose move to Cedar City increased the number of poets in a small southern Utah town exponentially and whose sharp eyes, intelligent and generous consultations, and sense of humor were invaluable in shaping this manuscript.

I give a special thank you to Andrew and Olivia for their love and support.

Finally, I want to thank my long-standing dear friends from my first writing group in red rock country—Kay Cook, Elise Leahy, Julie Simon—with fond memories of our Friday afternoon gatherings in Cedar City.

Contents

IV. Vespers in the Great Basin

Drift Migration happens when a migrating bird in flight
is blown off course by the winds.

To those who have drifted off course into new terrain—may you find your way.

Phosphenes

Close your eyes and they will soon appear—
small flashes floating in shadow as if you dove
below the photic zone where sunlight can't reach
and lantern fish send signals through bioluminescent scales.

Sometimes you see tunnels of green or yellow
that spin you through halos until you catch
a helix unraveling into ballet—
starlings in murmuration over fields in autumn.

It has been called the prisoner's cinema (the brain's trick
after days of four-walled darkness), phantom light projected
by cells firing in the retina, sighted by astronauts, pilots,

truck drivers—an aurora borealis or blizzard from the optic nerve.
Thick flakes pelt the windshield as the road narrows. You disappear
around a curve through the only passage you have ever known.

I

The Sand Man

Spies
hiss in the stillness, Hansel,
we are there still and it is real, real,
that black forest and the fire in earnest.
  —Louise Gluck, "Gretel in Darkness"

Drift Migration

Mother calms us with the story of two children
who live on a floating island: *In a glass-bottom boat*

they sail over anemones and sea urchins
to a coral reef where sting rays glide along the riffle,

translucent medusas with the low tide, their tentacles in seaweed . . . .
Our hands cramped around scissors

we cut out paper accordions of a girl and a boy.
My brother draws blue waves with a crayon and a boat.

A billboard: *Stardust Motel.* The exit sign: *Valley of Fire.*
Sand and creosote, broken bottles sparkling before his head

smashes the windshield near rows of telephone poles.
His name thrives in a desert as open as the sky

that rains down dry-throated gullies, soaks cleft mud flats.
His name lies flat on the grass near a copper vase filled

with flowers where the road ends in wind and Joshua trees.
I imagine him pulling a black vinyl album from its case—

Rust Never Sleeps. Bats fly on the only night I play his songs,
the only night the bats move in quadrangles.

The floor tilts toward me, sways into water,
and I see him sail past the coral reef to our own island.

Lighting Out for the Invisible

1.
Rush hour traffic threads the valley, suburban Ulysses taking his time—
my brother circles his scooter around the empty driveway,

waits for the Dodge Dart to pull up. Mother salts a casserole,
my brother and I play slapjack on the dining room table.

Third grade, my first glasses—blue tortoiseshell frames
in a red leather case stamped with a white lamb.

Mother unravels herself into remnants we skirt around
to disappear each into our own labyrinth.

She awakens from her sleep, turns on the light,
sees the walls are blue, the color of sky

when something falls through it—
a kite or balloon let go from a hand.

They give me birds' eyes and the grass and leaves
sharpen into needles of grass, leaf stems.

Even now my fingers fumble around the bedside table,
knocking over jewelry, the clock, so I can swim through the murky air.

2.
Sundays at Mint Springs we kick away silky reeds,
swim toward the dock where the sky falls over us,

my brother a blur diving for treasure
while Mother reads beneath the pines,

shades her sight with her hands
as my father disappears farther across the lake.

He turns his face away from his son's glassy eyes
to look too deeply into the water,

a fisherman's gaze lost in the net's silver,
blind to its breathlessness.

In my mother's house I wake to cold rooms;
the moon falls behind sandstone mountains.

Three o'clock, three-thirty (if my brother had
lived to be twenty), four o'clock, four-thirty—

I wait for the dawn to whitewash the houses
on my mother's street. It's been three years.

I sleep in his room—big muddy Pumas,
oil-stained jean jacket still in the closet.

3.
I watch through the telescope Saturn's rings,
the Orion nebulae like a flower bursting,

roses dropped beside the man selling pastel chalk.
I give him a dollar for a tin of purples, greens, yellows

and walk past his display, past my brother and me
uncovering Easter eggs hidden among delphinium.

This happens on August afternoons,
a lace curtain blown over the windowsill

while I salt cucumbers on the cutting board,
and wind lifts leaves toward an evening storm

that shakes the summer lights on the patio—
I awake with a start and shatter the glass.

Proteus Cabinet

Two children slosh muddy Keds in water,
unearth salamanders that burrow webbed toes in silt.

The boy will leave behind his smile in branches
when their mother calls them for supper,

baking bread, forgetting the salt.
They watch fireflies wink in the backyard woods,

bottle the light snuffed out by morning.
It was not as though the sister turned away

and her brother was gone through the wardrobe,
but that morning the salamander spread its toes deep

and would not come out. There was no salamander.
Only a creek and a brother.

Open the window to let in the sky.
He will still be there when you go looking.

The Sand Man

1.
This is the story of two children who wander into the desert
and see a burning bush—creosote—the oldest plant on earth.

The smell of it after rain is of railroad tracks crossing desolation,
passing all the lives scattered at the root of the chaparral.

The brother and sister have followed *him*—
the man who coaxed them toward a mirage

with the promise they would see God.
In the desert there are circles of seeds, tracks of snakeskin,

diadems of sunflowers crushed into a map.
He does not give them manna but hops and hashish.

He takes them into the desert that sparkles at first of crushed jewels.
The sand shifts, the diamonds cut their feet.

He takes them into the desert and says *hush*.
He is not waiting for them to grow up

but to soften and fatten by feeding them sweet things—
but no, that story belongs to two other children.

2.

The brother and sister are never very close except once at the beach
when they leave pennies on railroad tracks that run behind cottages—

Lincoln's face, the Capitol, flattened into diadems
they throw into the ocean and trade out for shells.

They walk along the shore on Sundays—
mother at church, father at the office—

scouring the beach for bits of conch or nautilus,
their loneliness woven into the grains.

They track sand into the house and watch the Brady Bunch,
the sun flaring into a copper penny, bright with the face of God.

End of summer, their parents pack the station wagon,
drive all night across the Mojave to kill the heat.

The brother and sister watch car lights stream across windows,
both hoping to see a shooting star,

but the children spin beneath the sky so quickly
they are the ones burning through space.

3.
They are too old for shooting stars by the time they find the desert.
They walk railroad tracks, leaping over ties, collecting debris—

bottle caps, buttons, coins, a bracelet—
what slips out of other pockets into theirs.

The first time they see the sand man, he is across the tracks,
holding a small bag of sand in his fist.

He spins the grains into a kaleidoscope:
garnet, black magnetite, green epidote, red agate,

feldspar, calcitite, silica, fossils,
bits of coral, sea urchins, foram shells.

He spins music on a turntable, snaps a dance with his fingers,
pulls a rainbow of scarves through a ring, shades them from the sun.

He shows how the city rises from its ashes
at dawn and disappears into a flame at night.

One night he whirls the kaleidoscope into a windstorm,
so strong the brother and sister can't hear each others' voices.

He pours fire down the brother's throat
and leaves him pushing grit between his teeth.

While the sister sleeps he steals her eyes
so when she wakes years later

she can't see the split
he left in her heart.

4.
The brother veers off the highway at the age of nineteen,
an empty bottle of vodka tipped beside him.

There is no cross on the shoulder where he crashes
into the valley of the sun, valley of fire, valley of the shadow of death.

There is no mark of the mirage
where the sand man left them without water.

There is sometimes rain, at other times voices,
and always wind carrying litter—bits of tinfoil

or newspaper lines, a witness to other lost lives.
There is no way to open the door to the sand man's eyes.

5.
She wants to remember what it was like to listen to the train
whistle and clack its wheels outside her window—

a night hot as knives circling her skin
never cutting the flesh for blood, just scraping small scars.

What freight did those cars carry in and out of the desert
on tracks that were like Jacob's ladder to her,

a conduit to a place beyond the nights she slept with her eyes open,
beyond the mirror each morning—her face closed as a stone?

6.
The city blooms into pools of blackness at night.
Millions of car lights open across the desert,

the sun shifts its glare farther west,
and tarmac snakes begin to cool down.

A constant tread wears away the skin,
breaking it into diamond chunks

and the sister drives through the city,
the sand man's voice whispering

Don't sleep, don't sleep
Don't meet your other self in the space behind your eyes.

She searches the dunes for prints from thirty years ago.
Wind abrades quartz shaping the inland sand seas.

Her brother is in all the grains—
it is his broken face she has been staring at.

The sounding dunes bellow with a deep call
and she sings back until the wind sows a seed

into her heart's cleft—the night blooming cereus.
It takes root in her septum, drinks from her vessels.

Vines begin to fill the chambers choked with sand—
they wait for the one night in a year to flower.

7.

She wanders through dead zones between creosote bushes
whose roots take in so much water, nothing else survives.

The waxy leaves and yellow flowers still look the same.
He's close, she whispers, as if her brother could hear.

But she is alone in the desert that once sparkled of jewels,
which she now sees are glass, tinfoil, beer can tabs,

ordinary objects she sifts through her fingers.
Was he really here? she wants to ask the boy

who threw pennies with her into the Pacific
before his eyes grew glassy with the sand man's breath.

But she lost him so long ago—she is now half a century—
so young compared to the chaparral of nearly 12,000 years.

If she thinks the legend never existed, does its power die?
But this legend has a man's voice, a man's body.

"He's here," she says to the rain that releases resin
from chaparral leaves burning with the scent of railroad ties.

8.
Tiny fronds pressed around the cereus stamen
push the outer petals to open in her heart.

9.
He appears as an ordinary man taking an evening walk
except for the small bag of sand he carries.

He looks at her as though no time has passed,
as though there is not one where there were two.

"I brought a special one for you," he says,
and opens his palm to show a star-shaped grain

made from the shell of the tiniest creatures.
Its six points are delicate, milky white.

She has never seen anything so beautiful and small.
She finally sees his hand for what it is and what it was—

a wasteland thriving on fragments of once-living creatures.
"You can't fill the scar from where you took the eyes to my heart," she says.

10.
There are some who wait all their lives to see
the Queen of the Desert bloom at midnight.

The phoenix falls into city lights burning for miles
and a crescent rises above the skyline.

Heady perfume opens across the desert
and she sees them all now:

ghost flower, evening snow, Venus shooting star.
Their grace thrives despite the arid soil.

She feels more than sees the moon-white petals
expand in her dark place of sand and blood.

The sand man's bag splits open
and all things past spill out of her heart.

It's only me she whispers to the boy
who wandered the tracks with her, as if he could listen,

and it is only her, the sister, leaving the desert.
She places a penny beneath the burning bush.

Sepulveda Basin Refuge

They congregate along the lake's shoreline—
snowy egrets, coots and grebes used to the noise

from the large, loud birds out of LAX that manage to fly so high.
A leaf blower scatters dry sycamore leaves along the footpath,

roaring over the only sign of winter in Los Angeles,
and someone's model airplane whines in the air.

Beer cans, bottles, plastic bags jam a creek below the asphalt trail—
scraps of white paper crumple like tiny cranes in the mud.

A blue heron finds a rivulet, rests her leg.

Ghost Flower

He rambles after the waitress takes my order
to the conversation of clinking glasses, margaritas,

about how he still gets drunk on Friday nights with friends
from grade school, calls one of his daughters to drive him

home across the city, though he doesn't see himself swaying
in the passenger seat when they drop him off and he dissolves

in the desert heat into crushed jewels and snakeskin.
He tells me he once almost drowned in Lake Havasu,

the earth's center exploding in his lungs, but it was Atlantis
he came back from, an imaginary city on asphalt beneath his high rise.

Other diners size up the menu, order the special, exchange details of their day—
I see how the sun has etched lines on his face into a nervous tic.

He pays the bill across from me, asks about my family,
my marriage, catches a call on his phone, says he has to go.

Your brother was messed up, he says in the parking lot,
I had nothing to do with it, and you—

I cast petals onto scorched pavement. He flares in that mirage
and I wonder what he lets himself remember.

One Shot

The night *The Deer Hunter* opened at Barracks Road Theater,
the place was so packed my family scattered, and I sat next

to two men who joked about the rats in the water cage
and laughed at the Viet Cong soldiers screaming at De Niro

to pull the trigger in Russian Roulette,
but when Christopher Walken put the pistol to his temple,

muttered "one shot" and sent a bullet through his skull,
when the last scene closed with a toast to that town's lost son,

the theater was silent except one of the men
beside me who wept into his hands.

In our neighbor's backyard that night a writer shot himself—
Breece D'J Pancake, whose stories told of fallen recruits

from West Virginia mining towns, their graduation photos
distilled in the memory of friends who stayed behind.

Next morning, I drove to high school past mist-covered farmland,
far away from those older brothers who left and never returned

except in sobs breaking over the ones who did
and a town too stunned to speak.

Leda

Those who walked here last summer
remember swans taking bread from startled fingers
or swan boats weighted with children paddling

between crowded banks. But no one saw beauty walking with death
among the rhododendrons. How he encircled his fingers
around her wrist and said so small. How they left the Public Garden.

How he took her home. The whistling swan flies beneath
a shroud of fog at September's close. Bereft of her flock's wild
clustered call, she journeys to warmer weather,

always somewhere beneath the rim of earth
or behind memory's horizon. Lost in a drift migration,
the wind tightens against the beating bay of her throat.

II

Eurydice's Mirror

The ceiling fan spins your childhood

The ceiling fan spins your childhood through the smallest sound—
moths tapping their bodies against the screen,

your father charting Cygnus in the August sky,
rain on the window late at night that follows you

into the eyes of children who have never heard rain,
the last thing your mother says to you before you know it is the last thing.

You chart journeys on maps, memorize legends, highways, train routes,
and when you follow roads beneath constellations

the sky becomes both land and sea for traveling animals.
You ride trains that cross rivers where landmarks

unfold on a face or an arm—a scar on the left cheek,
a red mole, a wrist inked with a swan.

A woman spins her grief into a flame
that you carry between your fingertips.

Your sinews of voice trace ruin and light in her palm,
each of your notes on her skin a moth singed by a star,

spiraling through shells to no more words—
only the ocean echoes in her cochlea.

Your treasures are marbles

Your treasures are marbles, matchbox cars, old maps,
fly fishing lures you find in the reeds.

Hers are shells, antler shards, acorns,
the tip of a raccoon's tail found in mulched leaves.

You give her what you value most—
a mayfly nymph broken off someone else's line.

She puts it with an antler bit, and they are two fragments
rattling together, one snapped off, one shed.

Somewhere the fisherman has unsnagged his pole
and the buck has grown back its rack.

When he startles the stag in a clearing
he is stunned by its frame.

When it lurches into the woods
he looks for a hint of pelt, weaves it into lures.

The children who have never heard rain

The children who have never heard rain
sleep in a hedged-in heart beneath stone.

Their eyes glint in the black glaze of a swan's iris
and in white sails across a lake.

They call to you with their laughter
but when you approach, only leaves and dragonflies.

She once fell asleep to a river

She once fell asleep to a river—
she floated on currents,

swirled in eddies, dizzy beneath stars;
she became its breath and took in silt,

she became its eyes and saw minnows, trout,
deer fur skipping the surface.

A lure flickered indigo
and she left behind her river home.

You taste sweet water when you drink from her lips,
she tastes snow and a thousand blackberries.

When she becomes your lover, she hears the notes
in your voice's flame—moths playing wildly with light.

When you become her lover, you are bound
to someone searching for ocean.

Deer tongue fallen apples

Deer tongue fallen apples, haunches taking shape in the dawn,
the only sound: soft mouths nudging open ripe skin.

Her fingers trace that scar where you were cut and released—
her eyes so quiet like acorn beneath an oak leaf—

and rests where your first hunger was nourished.
You cast a line over a wind rose in the river

—a rock reflecting light from all cardinal points—
to catch her hair with deer fur and iridescence.

A blue line on a map marks a river from city to coast—
an azimuth on parchment that winds indigo

across deerskin scraped clean, soaked in lime,
stretched dry and marked with catadromous migrations

of rivers through inked-in mountains, valleys, towns to the painted sea.
You touch her past on the vellum in a constellation of vanished cities.

She carries a sundial shell

She carries a sundial shell in her hand, its tip a gnomon.
Libra's scales follow the day's journey on a sundial—

the scales derived from the scallop Venus rode to the strand,
the only shell that crosses oceans, clapping two valves through spume,

a hundred eyes on its rim. St. James fell into the sea
and was buoyed by their mouths clinging to his clothes.

The scallop-shaped scar on her cheek is a pilgrim's sign,
as if all her days were held in one moment she glimpsed

out the corner of her young eyes while collecting shells—
her own life's helix curls into a carapace to land at this morning.

She sleeps in the folds of your shirt

She sleeps in the folds of your shirt—
you are traveling and she tosses between hours.

It has snowed, is still snowing over the backyard
and deer come out of the woods to lick salt rubs.

A full moon lights the half-apples of their prints.
She reads about ghosts who wander between paradise and hell,

their bodies bloated with hunger, their mouths shrunk to needles.
In the river she knew such appetite too full for her mouth.

Only one of you is telling this story.
No one will ever know who is body and who is shadow.

She uncovers antler bone

She uncovers antler bone hidden in deer fern,
fingertips pressing grief into the cartilage.

Your stories join on a shore where freighters
cross a lake that makes its own weather—

lifeguards muscle rowboats against the tide
beyond bathers plunging into the choppy water.

You roll up your jeans and you both wade
knee-deep into waves rocking like the sea.

Your fingers glance the swan on her wrist, leave prints
on a red mole, tiny rose, below her collarbone.

Gray breakers soak your pant cuffs.
I am memorizing you already you say.

She speaks on your last morning

She speaks on your last morning
as though stealing someone else's time,

saying how you both love trains—
windows framing backyards of clotheslines,

gardens, tool sheds, alfalfa fields,
a mill shooting steam into the summer air.

Neither of you knows as the windows change scenes
that the train is speeding faster,

the cars behind you unbuckling at each town
until yours is the only car moving,

and you are the only ones left.
Trees in the backyards change color,

fields become fallow, the grist mill shuts down,
and the sky turns white with winter constellations.

So many flowers

So many flowers and rain on the willows
as names of the dead call her back to the river.

Between brambles and furze you look for her,
blind to your tongue moving over her name.

You call her back to brambles and furze,
to the strands of deer hair you tie into flies,

to last year's bud scales
now filled with blossoms and leaves.

Behind her lies the wake of your nights
when you saw wind roses that were her eyes.

She hears the quiet sorrow in your cupped hands
filled with water from the river—

you drink and you drink and you drink.
It is not strange there, a mirrored world.

You have seen it before when your face reflects in an eddy
and you wonder, who is behind those eyes, that mouth—

if you could just see through the water looking back,
you would see her remembering the taste of snow.

When she first lay beside you

When she first lay beside you, you would not close your eyes
but watched her until your pupils drew her into a pool.

She floated there beneath the sun, swam into a waterfall,
and plunged into the deep. Only then did you close your eyes.

All things she loved rose from your song—
salt in a mollusk shell, the compass of an antler chip,

and the nights when the children who have never heard rain
returned pieces to the places from which they were lost—

severed bone made whole or a shell's hinge
sealed over the creature brought home again.

What she has given you

What she has given you is a way to pilot the distance
between memory and a river of roads.

You follow highways behind hills, factories, farmlands,
tired of wandering abandoned tracks, tired of wanting across time.

No trains pass your house now—
no whistle leads you out the window to the next town.

You unlatch a box of deer hair, pheasant hackles.
Hunched over the table lit by a green lamp

you secure the hook in the pedestal vice,
set the thread in the middle of the shank,

wrap it toward you then away, stopping at the bend in the hook.
You pinch pheasant tail fibers on the thread, tie them into place,

a tail and abdomen for the mayfly, using peacock herl for the thorax.
Moths tap inside the lampshade, spiraling the wrong way home.

She looks for the day

She looks for the day you rode the train past yellow stalks—
alfalfa fields that shimmered in the afternoon

when you cupped her chin and turned her face toward you.
You were her mirror—a blue sea in which she found not herself

but a boy looking up at her window, who memorized maps by flashlight.
She looks for you behind mirrors as if the river could break the glass.

The silver shows only one face with eyes that haven't slept for years—
she wanders past closed windows, stares at the alcove of your locked door.

She looks for you in stories between leaded panes, of an old father
weeping over his bound son before he finds the ram in the thicket.

When did the water freeze to glass? She turns away from
the mirror and watches your lamplight until dawn.

Clouds turn from white to gray to black

Clouds turn from white to gray to black
and while you sleep it pours, fish leaping for the false flies.

You dream you catch them all and lay them side by side—a silver shroud.
You think you have caught her when you hear laughter

but it is just voices next door from a party that has moved in from the storm.
You walk through the wreck of a train station, stepping over broken glass,

cracked bricks, graffiti, newspapers crumpled on the stairs.
Cygnus appears in the stars over the rusted tracks.

You can take her back in the darkness, she is not a dream—
her body against yours, her hair, cheek, lashes brushing your arm.

Don't open your eyes she whispers and you both drown in a braided river
but as you drown you rock each other as if you are riding a train

through a place no one else has entered.
You listen to the note only you have heard on the sinews of her voice,

a vibration of music so exquisite you must open your eyes—
your fingers hold moth wings burning in starlight.

III

Blood-Red Seeds

Night the trees trill at the edge of my ear,
a seven-year sleep unraveling
from husks honeyed to bark—
there was a night like this,
leaves slowly falling,
a year opening into rings and rings.

We skipped stones across them,
across the maple's reflection:
its fallen crown a ghost of leaves.
I took you into the waterfall where we drowned.
The narcissus opens like a dove
to the center of a sand dollar.

I reach for winged petals on the edge of flight.
The last note I hear is the sea's echo
sounding at the shell of my ear, your cry.
My first gift in a strange place—
six blue china horses,
a wilderness in their eyes.

He holds them in his hands as if holding the sea.
Take them, he says.
I touch their cool hooves.
Now you must always return.
I smash the horses into blue foam.
Deeper into the earth, I carry the sea with me.

Mother calls out my name
to the garland of flowers
spilled on the ground.

She strips away everything,
seeking only the core petal by petal.
She walks today over cracks in pavement,

whispers her grief
to pocks in concrete.
A contrail, white veil splits the sky.

The dawn flares behind branches in early bud—
the sky is red silk, color of the seeds
splitting open beneath my tongue.
I pack my car, drive over low grassy hills

away from him still sleeping and the sky is red silk
staining my lips as he reaches to touch the cold side of the bed.
The kindness of your eyes almost breaks the bond he forged
when he slipped the blood-red seeds into my mouth.

They branded my throat but your touch soothes their burn.
In all the years of awakening to spring,
in all my dread of returning to his cold body,
I had forgotten my thirst for your hands.

You tell me it rained a few days ago,
that in the evening you took off your suitcoat,
walked through the warm streets, the air damp
with the smell of old bricks and mortar.

The lilies you left on the table
open their speckled petals
and dark-tipped stamens to your voice.
You wandered every city that night.

I slice each stem on an angle
and heal the cuts in a vase of water.

Whether I lose you or find you again
the beautiful boys skimming waves on their surfboards
and slim girls braving the breakers will find each other one day
to watch their children dig faster as sea foam

bubbles through sand walls, fills a castle moat,
the day's half-moon anchored to the sky.
A girl releases a string, guides it with a taut pull
and the silken owl soars from her hands

above a shark kite smacking the air
with an upside-down smile of white teeth.
At night children run from behind lilac bushes,
the broad-leafed maple, the treble of cicadas,

and a boy calls out "All ye, all ye outs, in free!"
to bring the ones still hiding home—
then a white sail, geese flying south.
Their wings burn a moonless path.

In the kitchen mother says
nothing as she husks corn—
kernels gleam with centuries of autumns
we have seen come to an end.

My mouth—once filled with petals—
harbors a snowfield of grief.

I slip through a crevice beneath the crust of snow—
a pearl returning to the oyster's dark purse.

IV

Vespers in the Great Basin

Winter Solstice in the Gorge

Our myths turn long nights into cut evergreen
sold on grocery store parking lots, a continent away
from reindeer starving as the Arctic ice dissolves.
Only one star guides the way for diesels lit like Christmas—

miles of commerce that thread the Mojave.
The longest night spills from a cup of tears I drink
through this highway that weaves between monoliths
of an American Stonehenge along the Virgin River's winding course.

At the hour's cusp I see her face in the rock—
Freya who carries the sun in antlers. She spins a wheel
around our breath, seeds the earth with bits of amber.

At dawn the sun stands still on a plateau of Kaibab sediment,
reaches its rays down gypsum layers, touches sandstone
near big horn sheep who step out of shadow.

Utopia/Nowhere

Piano lessons over at dusk, I step into Fraternity Row
of boys drinking beers beneath Ionic columns
not knowing where to strike next before light fades
over Jefferson's serpentine walls wrapped around hidden gardens.

A drunken student drapes himself around a statue:
I love you Mr. Jefferson—I luuuve you!
The Chapel bell rings six times,
and maple leaves crunch under feet at the corner where

I wait for my mother, music books close to my chest,
a bite in the air on the last days of autumn,
my friend Libby, the next student, playing
the berceuse through the window.

Is this where Paris heard the goddess whisper,
"Choose me and I will give you Helen?"
And he—dim-witted boy—stole the careless king's wife
as she left behind what seemed a dream,

a shuttered beauty overgrown with ivy.
Libby quits lessons and becomes a faceless name
I tease off the canned pumpkin my mother scoops out for pie,
sees her father once a month at prison in Richmond.

And when she asks me over to her house,
I make excuses until she moves away
to live across the tracks at the end of a road
and joins a group of girls in tangy embers

who roll fingers over cigarettes on the football field
before stepping long-legged into the frat parties.
Her house disappears along with her father's name,
her mother's wedding ring, her spelling tests—

the girls flash their whispers over the field.

Arachne

She weaves all night the memory of girls
at the university dive where frat boys
eye their high school gleam of sundresses,

bare legs, sandals, where their tossed hair says
What else to do in this town after winning the game?
She weaves their hearts through indigo, vermillion,

piecing a stained-glass shimmer. Pierced by divine stare,
she shrinks into her body's new silk, weaves
shatters fine as hair undone on Sunday

morning, a long thread of weeping.

Flightless in Jefferson Country

Each morning Mike uses the bus route to the white neighborhoods,
past the bronze of Lee and Traveler in the downtown square,
past McIntyre Park, up Meadowbrook Heights into the subdivisions,
but I never go to the city center where he lives along Rose Hill.

On Fridays, my white friends and I walk arm-in-arm
to each other's homes across backyards for a glass of milk
to wash down E-Z Bake cake crumbles, while he boards the bus
with his older sister and the black kids from his neighborhood.

At Monticello, archeologists brush off broken crockery
found in the razed Mulberry Row—one cabin still remains,
a legacy of Sally Hemings who could never leave the "Little Mountain,"
questions about her children by Jefferson answered with glares as tour guides

marvel at the Venetian porches or the Seven-Day Clock designed
by the "man of his time." One morning Mike's mother sends him and
Antoinette to the corner stop then collapses of a heart attack.
We don't know what to do with his stares out the window or his blank face

at recess, so we forget his silence and play hopscotch and run away from
boys teasing for a kiss. Jefferson bought two mockingbirds from a man
his father-in-law enslaved, taught them to sing French tunes.
Decades later wild offspring would fill the woods with their song.

Antoinette drops out at 15. She's pregnant, names her son Rickus.
When she brings him to class for a visit, the teachers smile awkwardly,
don't say a word about the white guy in his twenties seen hanging around,
who parked on Rose Hill to capture a bird blown from the nest.

Leaving Virginia

Utah houses soften their angles at dusk,
hollyhocks blend with the larkspur.
Women disappear behind graciousness—
a smile that tells nothing.

Their shadows stretch in the twilight
that darkens a kitchen window.
They sweep out corners,
holding the wand of a broom.

Sand skims the patio beneath
a mirage of white dogwood petals.
I seem on the edge of everything—
the Mojave spread out west beyond

the grid streets of a Mormon town.
My first night in the desert,
stars I had only glimpsed through
a humid haze now glitter bright as ice.

Heliography

Listen—beneath a dogwood, I breathe in softly
and sing "I Wonder Where the Lions Are."
You wade into the creek. It's the song we play in your house
and use as a window through which I swim back to the dogwood and spruce.

You feed your neighbor's horse honeysuckle, apples,
cook dinner on the grill beneath pines,
your white husky trotting at your heels.
Who are you, wild and lonely, stroking my summer cotton dress?

Lightning takes me back to every place I've ever lost—
the water hole, pearly silt in the river, green espadrilles
drying in the sun while the vinyl spins with song.
I slip off my bathing suit. The sheets flutter beneath us.

You are a stranger and everyone I've ever met—
the same mouth on my lips and never touching them.
Sometimes I see a meadow when I cross the backyard
or pull Virginia creeper from the red bud—

crushed grass beneath the dogwood, fireflies,
where you carried a promise of something in your hands.
Was it a rock from the creek bed, a cluster of acorns?
You turn your face to glance back not believing

I've been behind you all this time,
but it's enough to throw me forward to this room
and traffic outside the window where the air is dry—
no glen tastes of wild roses, your mouth.

I've grown softer within a hardening shell you once un-spelled.

Metachrosis

Age six in Nairobi I pull off my shirt after school,
brown my small chest in an antelope sun,
smooth my blonde legs on the yellow dust plain.

At recess British boys tease me about my American accent—
watch out, she's going to cry—and at night I chant
the name of the boy next door, Kebaki Kebaki.

Outside my window, Argus-eyed chameleons shift
from gray to green to blue, cling to branches
with their toes, curl their tails into vines,

while I pretend wild flamingos stretch across
my palm pressed into the sand of Mombasa Beach
where jelly fish float their balloon bodies in low tide.

Ten years later in Virginia woods,
a bird's fluted keening rises from mimosa fronds,
thin like the gazelle's trembling whistle,
soft through its nose in the thorny Kenyan brush.

Shadow Prints

We wait to sight a black leopard beneath a constellated sky
after my father pulls the Land Rover up to a copse of moringa trees,
cuts the engine, shines a light into branches at two in the morning,

I am ten, fidgeting in the car, tricked into thinking I see a tail,
a sleek paw, but the dark body never shows itself.
I fall asleep as we drive back to our tent, and dream of Kebaki Kebaki,

the boy next door who pretends he is Sinbad to rescue me from sea monsters
swimming across his backyard to the rock where I stand.
Back in the States, you are already seventeen,

working your first summer job as valet at casinos on the Strip,
while I am a few miles away from the equator,
skip over it like a jump rope in my British uniform,

striped orange and white like a Creamsicle, recite the Lord's Prayer
in Assembly, then pledge allegiance to the Queen. We never find
the leopard, but see cheetahs, gazelles on the grasslands.

You spend nights cooling off in Las Vegas,
a city called "the meadows," draw a high draft number,
drag Tropicana with the windows rolled down.

Later I move west to your desert, bring the leopard with me,
watch with her eyes as you dive into a pool, glide the length of your body
over racing stripes before lifting your head to take a breath—

just as she had watched us, alert beneath the Milky Way,
camouflaged in the tree's canopy, muscles tense
and ready to spring if the scent of human got too close.

Daedalus Bookshop

Scrolls of feathers hold a sun painted on the wooden sign
at the shop's door on Fourth and Main that opened
when I was a child to hard-bound copies of *The Little Princess* and *Bambi*.
In high school I followed musty books through each room,

shelves circling tighter around those hours held in the place
where memory curls in folds of the brain shaped like a ram's horn,
(named after the Egyptian God Amun "the hidden one").
There at fifteen I found James Agee's *Collected Poems*.

Borges imagined the Minotaur hunted him through a labyrinth—
lines he shaped into an architecture of his wandering.
He heard its voice bellow from depths in the Horns of Ammon.
Or was it the horns calling him back from the hunt?

The ancient architect flew to another land, rarely recalled
the son he lost to the sea, as Agee did on page five
where I first read, August 1978,
"Little child take no fright

in that shadow where you are," when I paid
the two dollars and stepped out
from the dark corridors into the sun.

Vivarium

All other days collide
like fireflies in a mason jar.
But that day on the mountain

when you left your hat,
drove back through flurries,
retraced your steps along the ridge,

found it behind the fallen tree
where we had picnicked the week before—
that day breathes through holes stabbed into the lid.

I watch the snow fall more thickly out my window,
vaguely answer a friend's question:
"Yes, yes—let's look into that . . ."

and map a future in pencil on ridges
of graph paper of you and me—
snow in a mason jar.

We live in parallel lives across town.
On some days you might as well be out to sea
or a castaway on Circe's island,

but you are only leaving the grocery store
or stuck in traffic on Main Street
while I stand at the front window

and wait for so much unopened mail.
The same raven struts along the curb,
cocking its head when I leave home.

I have been told they recognize faces—
this one has watched me for months.
Circulars pile up on the dining room table.
I swear he looks at me with human eyes.

Kaleidoscope

So many rectangles in this house—
the couch, the doorway, the transom above the entrance,
the coffee table with a ceramic vase of swirled colors

an old boyfriend bought for me from a Boston vendor.
He bundled it in newspaper, then a paper bag, strapped it to the back
of his motorcycle, showed up all in black—

leather chaps, jacket, sunglasses. We steamed clams,
dipped them in butter, while we sat on rotting wicker
in a screened back porch and a cooling storm blew through.

I laughed about the vase, his hair wild from the storm,
his new job as a roadie for Aerosmith—their *"Permanent Vacation*
drug-free come-back tour"—but he got fired at Christmas,

called me drunk and crying, though by then I had found you,
standing in the alcove of my new place in Utah.
Friday night—I'm watching "America's Most Wanted."

The landlady had told you, *she never goes out, she's always alone.*
You showed me the Pleiades, Cassiopeia, Mayfly nymphs under rocks
of a landscape spun purple, turquoise, ecru, colors of a desert

that erodes the past, though a screen of rain falls through the glaze.

Venus

My grandmother watched one blue afternoon
huge waves roll toward the rocks in Monterey Bay,
lunge over the 40-foot sea wall, break at beds of ice plant,
the surge flooding the road, spray striking her window in the cottage

she bought when Cannery Row was still a cannery.
A few hours later police stopped to tell her an earthquake
hit Alaska and sent a tsunami to Pacific Grove—
she never got word it was too dangerous to stay.

Fifty years later on my walk along the sea wall,
clouds brood over black water splashing rocks
where boat lights plumb the surface below the cliff

and otters sway in their sleep on kelp beds.
She said it was the most beautiful thing she had seen,
a wave traveling for miles to break shells at her doorstep.

Snow in March

It falls around streetlights, confetti for a voyage
none of us are taking, curled in sleep as we are,
beside a lover breathing or holding tight to our own chest

beside no one. It fills the crooks of ash and apple trees,
contours sharp angles of roofs across the street,
weighs down hundred-year-old spruce.

On the couch, my white cat keeps warm in an old blanket—
he is feather-light and dying. The angles of his haunches
and spine fold into my arms as if he were a kitten again.

It's 4:00 a.m. I set the dryer and think of my grandmother
climbing up and down the stairs. A widow for years,
she once asked me to write a poem about a December bride,

snow on trees like a satin dress and lace veil. But this night
the flakes are a veil of moths covering each street candle.
We dream the bride from our beds, and she is all one—

my grandmother arranging damp sheets in the dryer,
the white cat who sleeps his last breaths on the sofa.
I move my pen across paper in the dark as if gliding
across ice at midnight, not even feeling the cold.

Old Haunts

Cicadas trill outside my open window
but it's only crickets rubbing their legs in the Utah night.
Their song tricks me back down the path across the stream
to McIntyre Park where high school friends take their children

on the Fourth of July. Red, copper, blue fireworks flash with a boom
then whistle into sulphur and ash as small hands wave sparklers
over blankets, and magnesium burns slowly above a child's wrist
into emptied KFC buckets. I stand at the cul-de-sac of my old house,

where the blue spruce stretches its shadow over the groove my bike
wore in the grass, and watch new owners set the dining room table
then switch on lamps to play a record that spins vibrato through the walls,
before I fall back to sleep this side of the Continental Divide.

Memory at Taylor Creek

—After the drawing by Eric Brown

I disappear into the fallen tree damming the creek
or into a dark flock of ravens settled on branches,
or even into your eye as a boy, filled with a stag's belly

blocking the sky, hooves and antlers a blur.
I balance on a rock in the creek, fling out my arms—
the bracelet on my wrist falls into the stream,

glints turquoise out the corner of my days. Twenty years later
you retrieve it from the cold silt and coil it in my palm.
Each uprooted branch sends me beyond the crags

where I find an antler chip—bone the color of ash.
You were left on your back, falling, inverted, supine
watching the deer leap over you—its arc a messenger

whispering *take this home with you.*
So you take split hooves, cracks in the rock,
black wings in flight or claws curled around bark

until you paint what is visible—yellow and cerulean blue.
We return to a house full of treasures,
swans gathering rain on their wings, a feather between fingers,

your name a ripple spread into rings telling the age
of a tree planed into a headboard,
pillows propped against the grain—the life we've grown into.

Augury

We don't know how to read the strange cairn on the river trail—
sticks propped over stones, a message for another hiker.
But not for the man with his black Lab bounding ahead
then trotting back to nose his hand, gait certain of immortality.

Nor the boy whistling as he slips into the woods and adjusts his backpack.
A woman lopes with her walking stick, adds a rock to the pile
and clatters up the path toward dusk. "Moon kissed," I whisper
to the scent in your shirt collar. The bear rises overhead

in the eastern sky. And we stop short—a snake lies still on the path,
head resting against dirt, narrow tail camouflaged in brambles,
body frozen until her jaws sense our footsteps tread away.

Circadian

Small things undo me—the dishwasher's cycles,
the clock's tick, the ceiling fan's hum.
Three in the morning the clock stops.

I've dusted and swept the room, lifted each knick-knack,
but overlooked a sheen on the coffee table.
Highway traffic whines through the open window.

A gray cat minces down the stairs.
We all disappear and reappear in some form—
I pass myself in wisteria vines wrapped around the porch,

and you are in the train whistle heading out of town.
My body lets in light as I stand in the kitchen, startled by long division,
spiders that move like quick shadows in corners,

the weight of the day on my shoulder seeking something
beyond afternoon light crossing linoleum, something finer
than contrails, or laundry on the line beside a hedge of wild roses.

At dusk tiger moths drink from night flowers,
click their tymbals to block the sonar of circling bats,
and I remember when I was twelve I danced to the *Firebird*

in the living room on winter evenings—the record player spun the oboe
as I spiraled to my image in dark windows, en pointe in snow.
I circle back to that night where the needle roves the vinyl

until it scratches the label, and the girl slides the music
into its sleeve, switches off the lamp, watches flakes catch fire
beneath the porch light, where I now stand in August.

Retrieval

Air in the empty chambers of the ammonite
gives it buoyancy for swimming
until it settles in sediment as the Kaibab sea
shrinks from the Great Basin that is so deep,
its rocks and shells will never reach the ocean.
The ocean will have to come to them,
pouring over the rim when the west coast
sinks into depths that flood the Mojave.
In another epoch, creatures in limestone
will taste this new salt abrading
their locked beds—a trail toward home.

Great Basin

I am no nearer to what the sea tries to loosen wedged in rock—
a sorrow slipped between a trapped metal cap
and glass shattered along another coast.
The truth is I don't live near the ocean

but in a desert town I refuse to see
built on an alluvial fan of gypsum soil shifting
beneath cracked plaster and skewed door frames;
beneath miles of silver sage, rabbit brush, dry lakes

and wind trembling through pinyon rooted along the highway
that stretches through Paiute land. I leave my own trace,
planting wisteria, honeysuckle—southern foreigners thirsting for water.
I blink and the town is gone, drowned in a sea of fossils.

What that sea left behind is the desert I walk through,
a sorrow slipped between trilobites and shale.

Desert Insomnia

Truckers roar southbound past harbors of lights—
who lives in those towns?—
before fading into the Virgin River Gorge,
headlights scanning crags for big horn sheep.

They mark their time by Shell Stations and bluffs outlined in the dark.
I listen at midnight to the distant whine from my front porch—
a cloud sits on its haunches over a plain of stars.
All summer the child next door clicks and chatters

grace notes to the crickets' calls, her days filled with faces
she can't decipher, colors and noises that set her mind spinning.
But on some nights, she echoes the music she hears—insects humming,
whoosh of sprinklers, highway engines. I rock myself to sleep to her chimes.

Quietus

The ones we've lost were cut loose so easily
as if the slightest wind undid their stems,
their voices silent, though we have spilled the black
blood of a thousand lambs into the soil of Erebus.

Yet we remain here locked in our skulls,
curling and uncurling fingers around toothbrushes,
pencils, forks. The next wind will come tonight,

tomorrow, next year, or decades from now when the spruce,
barely two feet, dwarfs the barn. And what of you,
my own Ulysses, who fought no one
to reach my bed of antique brass, not olive trunk?

Who now sleeps, the breath of your life a sigh in the hallway.
Together we wander this strange house—
conscious as marble, sonorous as dirt.

Vespers in the Great Basin

Bald eagles gather among the elms with soft whistles
as they glide over snowfields of thistle and jackrabbits,
settle on branches, umber wings folded against their bodies,
albino heads tucked from the wind. Each winter we watch them

fly across the valley to this empty ranch, stretch their wing-span beyond six feet,
their darkness growing in sunset until Venus appears in the west.
Driving home, your right hand fumbles with my fingers
as if with a rosary, while your left keeps the wheel in check.

Out the window I see a brown quarter horse lean against a fence in snow,
haunches turned to the wind. Our silence meets the coldness that blows in
through doorjambs, the chimney. Next January when mountain peaks glisten
beneath miters of ice we'll return to the elms as eagles gather across the river

and the riven valley—they'll hunch together on racked branches
of winter trees, still believing they can keep the cold at bay.

The Glass Blower

We follow the Spanish Trail past Bunkerville,
a town that harbored fall-out to its bones,
a road that dips and rises along hills,

then crosses I-15 and disappears north to Caliente
where we look out the window at miles strung between telephone poles.
Years have narrowed our eyes into the couple at the casino breakfast

who study laminated menus to order the "Deuces Special"—
2 eggs, 2 slices of bacon, 2 sausage links, 2 pancakes.
We don't say a word while we eat.

The asphalt glints of mirages and we are sure
that if we just drive over the next crest
there will be an oasis clear enough to drink.

The setting sun turns the hematite of red hills molten in its crucible,
spins shells of animals long since gone into sandstone.
I remember in high school the artist at the mall

who shaped molten glass into cats curled on a mirror
or deer grazing suburban shelves. Each week I returned
to choose a different hand-spun creature.

The menagerie still sleeps in bubble wrap
—rabbits, lambs, foxes—stored in our basement,
near volcanic glass collected from dormant peaks.

Two peach-colored kissing birds crested our cake topper
but broke in the last move. I walk a labyrinth west of town,
place my old *Self* at the center, retrace the path out the rock circle,

and face renewal across the playa of an ancient shoreline.

All Fever Gone

A storm over sandstone hoodoos obscured Bryce Canyon's sharp blue sky—
we sheltered in a rock alcove beneath black clouds, our shirts
soaked with rain, your lips browsing the nape of my neck.

Then thunder flashed. We never knew how close lightning struck.
The others waited inside the lodge—your sister, her fiancé.
At her wedding, we slipped away past the gazebo

disappeared into trees like deer, like foxes, skipped over river rocks,
and lay on the other side until the night shed cold stars.
We returned for toasts, dancing, cutting of the cake

when her husband smashed red velvet into her mouth, licked it off.
Years later we meet off I-15 at Fort Deseret, take photos of each other
in door frames of old dugouts, adjusting apertures for light.

This is the country where I remain, all fever gone, or slipped
between volcanic peaks and Triassic hills into a land
charted by arches, pinnacles, layers of black basalt.

In the matte print, you lean your shoulder against adobe walls—
behind your smile, the miles of desert beyond the Confusion Range touch
the Nevada border and reach me thirty years later putting dishes away.

Palimpsest

1.
We were a strange coupling in the skeletal frame
of the house we trespassed near the highway.
You carried me piggy-back across the threshold

and I stuck my head through the unfinished window
overlooking the yard's debris: broken bricks, a fire pit,
clay pigeons shot into half-moons.

Neon signs flickered across the valley
—*Little Wonder Café*—
your mother waits tables, 1948,

boys she knew back from the war,
generous tips and offers
all ghosts now.

2.
We have been apart so long, I can't give you back that day.
I can only wish us into another framed window
where dusk mutes the swings in the backyard,

and we watch our children pump their legs
higher into the air until they fade beyond sight.
We are still asleep beneath the roofless sky

in that bedroom of plywood and tar paper walls
where we dream of old bullet shells, cracked terracotta,
and scorched rocks burning a million years into our hands.

Hollow Bones

I used to watch storms darken Three Peaks, facing the wind
that blew veils over volcanic domes, ranch lands, sage brush
to where I stood on the edge of lava rocks, calling your name to the valley

as if my voice could reach where you slept on the other side of the country,
drowning in buses and rain, before I returned home to music that replayed
our walk on South Street in Philly—another city we shared.

On the morning I heard you had died, I drove to those hills
in mid-January, steered over rutted roads to an old shooting range.
A red-tailed hawk rested on the tallest boulder, didn't move

except to shift her head when I clicked the car door shut
and walked close as she would let me.
I surveyed snowfields, ranches, my life until her scream

and tan-spotted wings glided on cold air,
folding into a speck below,
talons perched on bud scars dormant until spring.

I sleep behind drawn shades and live on a thread of want,
a necklace strung with wooden animals—leopard, rhino, giraffe.
They cock their ears toward snoring from the room next door.

Things take shape in the dawn—halogen lamp, basket of letters, a closed door.
To think of where I stood at your threshold on the brink of going inside.

Flight Path

The view from my front porch is a white stucco house,
its dark dining room, windows back-lit,
and a blue half-moon of television glow.

Cottonwoods and spruce stand above the roof,
so high they block the sunset as hawks
circle from fields to roost in branches.

I imagine that I fly beyond the trees over
a hill of mansions, a dry lake, sage brush,
until I clear the dormant volcanoes of Three Peaks,

cross the border where I follow Basin and Range,
Sierra Nevada, Great Valley, toward the dark Pacific.
But now the porchlight flares across the street—

a man says goodbye to the neighbors,
thanks them for dinner and opens his car door,
as they close and latch theirs,

flick off switches, leave the one to shine.

Metamorphic

Wind still blows across the desert with lightning and hail
crushing delphinium, hyacinths, flowers not native to the West—
their blooms too bright for the muted striations that flank the town.

But morning light sets fire to red cliffs on the east hills
where time is compressed into a gray stripe of marine traces—
Triassic, the oldest layer of the shoreline, parallels Main Street.

Perhaps it is too much to carry two places at once.
The weight of the home left behind presses against the walls of this one
as if the Appalachians hiding stories of their age beneath oaks, mossy stones,

thickets wild with ferns, could sheer the red-rock cliffs of legends until their layers
disintegrate into a basin of salt from the dogwood blossom's hard, green tears.

Evensong

Sunbeams scatter through oxygen and nitrogen
bending frequencies into a band of blue, gray and white
swallowed by waves of nautical twilight,
the moment Venus appears next to

Algol the demon star, and Lambda—
astral boat lights floating on the January horizon.
I fly over arteries of lights in a brasilia,
tilt to one side along the Buckhorn Flats.

Home is scattered: red cliffs to the east,
a dry basin to the west, and in between,
a town of three exits where I have lived out
the same day for 30 years. A glossy magazine

promises vacations to Denmark, Bali, Alaska,
where oceans beat the shores with breakers
from our first breaths before our lidless eyes
could no longer see through water.

At a wind gap, symbols on rock carved by
Fremont Indians tell of the equinox,
rain, a journey, a woman giving birth.
Cirrus clouds over the Pine Valley Range

must mean thunderheads building in Nevada.
They should reach us by tomorrow night.

Petroglyphs at Parowan Gap

All things crisscross before they disappear into a silence
throbbing between jutted rocks. A trucker drives on a road

perpendicular to the wind gap, visible for a moment, then gone.
A Pontiac guns from the closest town, swerves toward me, honks,

and the men spin away, laugh at my startled jump—I give them the finger.
We break the reverie summoned from eons of layers that streak rock

masked with graffiti. Names trespass a map carved five centuries ago in sandstone:
notches, ladders, a sun-circle of concentric rings that gives passage to the next traveler.

If we live in dreams, our eyes opening and closing to vistas we create
unless we step into someone else's meditation, then which ancient one

dreamt this intersection of lines—the distant trucker, the men, and myself,
who wander past a length of road into spirals so carefully engraved?

Our crossing notches a groove in my palm—a new map I now see in my hands.

Notes

"Daedalus Bookshop" was written in honor of Heather Heyer who was killed on Fourth Street in downtown Charlottesville, Virginia, protesting the Unite the Right rally on August 12, 2017.

"Memory at Taylor Creek" was inspired by Eric Brown's artwork *Memory from Taylor Creek*. The phrase "falling, inverted, supine" is a direct quotation from the Artist's Statement.

The epigraph from "The Sand Man" is a quotation from Louise Gluck's poem "Gretel in Darkness" published in *The House on Marshland*.

The Brasilia in "Evensong" refers to an EMB 120 Brasilia, a pressurized turboprop airplane with a capacity for 30 passengers.

About the Author

Danielle Beazer Dubrasky (she/her) received an MA in English/Creative Writing from Stanford University and her PhD in creative writing from the University of Utah. Her poetry has appeared in *Chiron Review, South Dakota Review, Ninth Letter, Pilgrimage, saltfront, Sugar House Review, Cave Wall, Open: Journal of Arts & Letters, Under a Warm Green Linden,* and *Terrain.org.* Her chapbook, *Ruin and Light,* won the 2014 Anabiosis Press Chapbook Competition. Her poems were also published in a limited-edition art book *Invisible Shores* by Red Butte Press of the University of Utah. She has been nominated three times for a Pushcart Prize and twice for Best New Poets, and she is a three-time winner of the Utah Original Writing Competition for poetry. She is also the co-editor of *Blossom as the Cliffrose: Mormon Legacies and the Beckoning Wild* (Torrey House Press). Originally from Charlottesville, Virginia, Danielle lives in Cedar City, Utah, homeland of the Paiute Indian Tribe of Utah Cedar Band of Paiutes. She teaches poetry at Southern Utah University and directs the Grace A. Tanner Center for Human Values as well as an annual Eco-Poetry and the Essay Conference.

Ashland Poetry Press

The mission of the Ashland Poetry Press is to publish and promote the best poetry submitted from new and established authors writing in English as well as translations of Spanish poetry into English. Editor's Choice selections include the following.

Danielle Beazer Dubrasky, *Drift Migration*, 2021

Marjorie Stelmach, *Walking the Mist*, 2021

David Mills, *Boneyarn*, 2021

Miho Nonaka, *Museum of Small Bones*, 2020

Heather Hallberg Yanda, *Late Summer's Origami*, 2019

Michael Miller, *Asking the Names*, 2017

Richard Jackson, *Out of Place*, 2014

Nicholas Samaras, *American Psalm, World Psalm*, 2014

John Hennessy, *Coney Island Pilgrims*, 2013

Richard Jackson, *Resonance*, 2010

Christine Gelineau, *Appetite for the Divine*, 2010

Michael Miller, *The Joyful Dark,* 2007

Scott Withian, *Arson & Prophets*, 2003

Kathryn Winograd, *Air into Breath*, 2002

William Sylvester, *War and Lechery*, 1995

Harold Witt, *American Lit*, 1994

Andrew M. Greeley, *The Sense of Love*, 1992